BIGFOOT Boy

INTO THE WOODS

Kids Can Press acknowledges the financial support of the Government of Ontario, through the Ontario Media Development Corporation's Ontario Book Initiative; the Ontario Arts Council; the Canada Council for the Arts; and the Government of Canada, through the BPIDP, for our publishing activity.

Published in Canada by
Kids Can Press Ltd.
25 Dockside Drive
Toronto, ON M5A 0B5

Published in the U.S. by
Kids Can Press Ltd.
2250 Military Road
Tonawanda, NY 14150

www.kidscanpress.com

Edited by Karen Li and Samantha Swenson
Designed by Rachel Di Salle

The hardcover edition of this book is smyth sewn casebound.
The paperback edition of this book is limp sewn with a drawn-on cover.
Manufactured in Shen Zhen, Guang Dong, P.R. China, in 4/2012 by Printplus Limited.

CM 12   0 9 8 7 6 5 4 3 2 1
CM PA 12   0 9 8 7 6 5 4 3 2 1

Library and Archives Canada Cataloguing in Publication

Torres, J., 1969—
        Into the woods / written by J. Torres ; illustrated by
Faith Erin Hicks.

(Bigfoot Boy)

ISBN 978-1-55453-711-2 (bound)   ISBN 978-1-55453-712-9 (pbk.)

        I. Hicks, Faith Erin II. Title. III. Series: Bigfoot Boy.

PN6733.T67I56 2012   j741.5'971   C2012-900560-6

Kids Can Press is a *l©rus*™ Entertainment company

BIGFOOT Boy
INTO THE WOODS

J. Torres and Faith Erin Hicks

Kids Can Press

For Titus, my little bigfoot.
Love, Da

For my brothers, who are now Bigfoot Men — F.E.H.

Friday ...

Saturday ...

Hi, there. You must be Rufus.

!

I'm Aurora. Your grandmother told us you'd be visiting.

I've seen your picture, but I didn't know your hair was so red in person. It's cool!

41

42

51

Gasp! You weren't attacked by that bear, were you?

Bear? What bear?

Actually, I'm not sure it was a bear. It didn't sound like one. But it was *big* like one.

I didn't really get a good look at it ... because I was running away ... but it kind of looked like ...

This! Where'd you get the totem?

Totem? What totem?

Enough of that already!

... don't give him the totem! You can invoke the rule of finders keepers!

Who is this flying rat?

The name's Sidney, Mr. Big Bad. And I know the "laws of the jungle." So to speak.

They know about the magic. They won't let Penny go unless I give them the totem. What should I do?

Personally, I'd never trust a wolf, eh?

Stay out of this, rodent. I have never tasted squirrel before, but there is a first time for everything.

Told you.

90

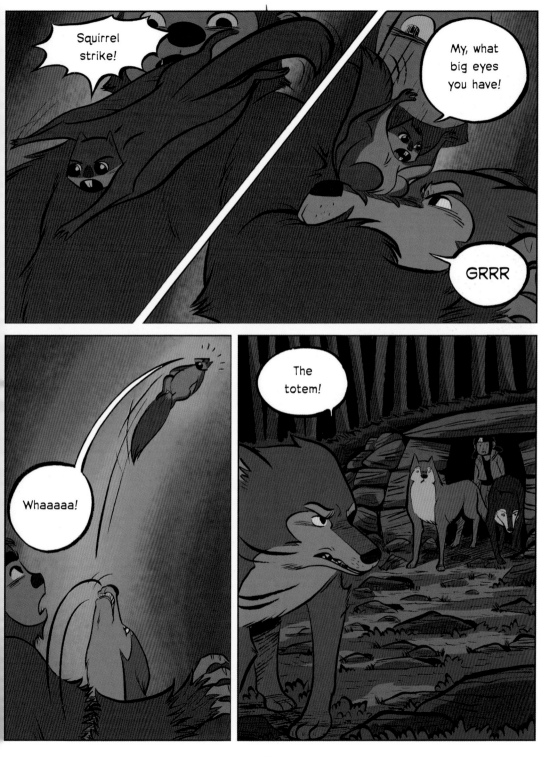

97